WILL YOU WALK WITH ME?

WRITTEN
BY
GWENDOLYN LEWIS
OCTOBER, 2024

Brothers-Womack Publishing, LLC
Flint, Michigan 48503
Printed in cooperation with KDP.

Print ISBN: 979-8-9856462-5-2
Paperback

Dedications

I dedicate my poems to ALL who have walked in my PATH -GUIDING, EVALUATING AND OFFERING OPPORTUNITIES.

Special Emphasis goes to..

John & Carrie Warren: My Parents (deceased)
Bruce & Pennet Warren:
My Brother and Sister in-law (deceased)
Gary & Darlene Lewis:
Brother in-law and Sister in-law

Joseph Alan Lewis: Son
Callet Warren: Niece
Karen Young
Katie Felton
Susan Beckford
and
the Computer Technicians
at the Redford Township District Library

To my husband,
JOSEPH BYRON LEWIS
(Deceased)

You inspired me to be the best I could be.
You gave me the space where I could grow.
I humbly, deeply, thank you for all you
have
done for me and our family.

"To GOD I Give The Glory"

WILL YOU WALK WITH ME?

MANY HAVE WALKED WITH ME-

Many have walked with YOU TOO.......

Greetings,

Walk with me as I share from my heart-
my loves, my joys, my sorrows, and my
travels.

These poems are conversations I had
with God.
They have helped me.
Hopefully they will inspire you
to challenge yourself and transpose your
life.

Gwendolyn Regina Warren Dudley Lewis

TABLE OF CONTENTS

Section 01

INSPIRATIONAL JOURNEY

Section 02

PACK A LITTLE KINDNESS

TABLE OF CONTENTS

Section 03 ADVENTURES ALONG THE WAY

Section 04 TRAVELING COMPANIONS

Section 05 MEET THE POET

Section One

Inspirational Poems

CAN I WALK WITH YOU?

(Dedicated To All Who Have WALKED In My Life's Path)

Can I walk with you?
I want to be a part of your life.
You share so many memories of my past.
You have a way of making me think,
To check myself,
To encourage me to be the best that I can be.

Can I walk with you?
You inspire me,
You taught me to ask questions.
I use to read and follow up and up and up
I use to sing, and sing and sing
I now fight for my deliverance,
I use to strive for acceptance,
I now strive not for acceptance but for knowledge,
guidance and truth.

There are so many people who have aided me
in this journey,
Males, Females
Blacks and White.
It been a journey.
It’s going to be a journey
Precious Lord, take my hand…Lead me on I will stand.
Standing on two feet…To go where you want me to go.
Lead me, guide me along the way.
Can I walk with you?

April 8, 2021

grl

WE WANT TO MAKE IT.

We all want to make it-
Even the man with the sign.
Did you see the woman crying
As you passed her by?
I don’t know if I can help her,
My load is heavy too.
We all going to make it,
Just hold on.
HOLD ON. HOLD ON!!

September, 2018

grl

DO YOU SEE ME?

Do You See Me?

DO YOU SEE ME!!

Do you see me in my journey called life?
Do you know what problems I have?
Stand by me.
Walk beside me
Until I make it there.
My journey is not far,
My journey is not long.
I can make it
If I don't have to make it alone.
Alone, Alone,
I can make my journey if I don't have to make it alone.

grl

“SEEK ME FIRST”

“All you have to do is SEEK ME FIRST
And all things I will give to you”.
If you want a car,
“SEEK ME FIRST”.
If you want a house,
“SEEK ME FIRST”.
If you want to travel,
“SEEK ME FIRST”
I say all you want,
I’ll give to you.
“SEEK ME!!
I’LL BE TRUE TO YOU.
If you are figuring out a life,
“SEEK ME FIRST.”
If you’re looking for a husband or a wife,
“I’ll be your mate until you set the date.”
“SEEK ME FIRST!!

May 18, 2024
Leaving De Gauile Airport..Paris, France

grl

HOW LONG?

How long have I been on this journey
called Life?
It is short lived you'll see.
Prepare for the journey,
It's not long in his eyes
You will see a difference in me.
The journey is up,
The journey is down.
Around the corner you'll see.
Men, women, girls and boys speeding by
Without a swish of knowledge
of who they will be.
Take time, leave a mark, it is short lived,
The journey to where we call home.

grl

HOW DO WE DO IT?

They say there's a purpose
To everything we do.
Can we really do what he wants us to do?
What does he want?
He says it in his book,
"LOVE ALL AS I FIRST LOVED YOU"
Can I fulfill my purpose?
Is it that important?
How do I do what's important to me?
Listen.
I'll tell you
It's as simple as that.
Reach out to God,
Help One another,
Know that he is with you,
He'll tell you what to do.
Sit Back, Study, Pray and follow HIS WAY.
They say there's a purpose
To Everything we do.
Do as I have commanded you…
To LOVE everybody as I do.

1980

grl

GET UP!!

YOU GET TO A POINT..

YOU GET TO A POINT..

You must be inspired to get UP!!

Get UP....... Get UP

For what?

You must be inspired to get UP!!

You need a place to go,

People to see,

A child to help,

A helping hand for yourself.

Get UP....... Get UP

Who do I help?

Who do I account for?

Who really care?

Get UP to sing,

Get UP to pray,

Get UP, Get UP, Get UP.

But, you need a reason to get up,

Come and inspire me to GET UP!!

HELP!

October 18, 2018

grl

IMPRESSION

Step up and impress GOD.
Impress God in everything that you do.
Step up and impress GOD!
In all that you do.
Thank him for the things he does,
The people you meet,
And the lives he touches.
Stand up and impress GOD!
For every waking minute
Whatever you say and do,
Stand up and impress GOD!!
Give God the Glory..
Ask him what to do.
He says,
“Love your mate as you love your church”-
“Do unto others as you wish for them to do for you”.
Show Love.
Stand Up And Impress
With Everything You Say or Do!!

grl

CAN I HAVE A MOMENT OF YOUR TIME?

Can I have a moment of your time?
I have alot to say.
I have alot to say
About this world,
About life…
Can I have a moment of your time?
I want to tell you that-
“LIFE IS SHORT”.
Do the right thing.
We don’t know what life will bring.
Go back and share your loves.
Go back and share your joys.

CAN I HAVE A MOMENT OF YOUR TIME?

April, 2020

grl

EVERYTHING IS GOING TO BE ALRIGHT!!

Everything is going to be alright.
All you have to do is TRUST in the LORD
with ALL your might.
Everything is going to be alright.
You broke your leg... IT WILL HEAL.
He broke your heart ...
TIME WILL TAKE CARE OF ITSELF.

'CAUSE,
EVERYTHING IS GOING TO BE ALRIGHT.
YOUR BILLS
YOUR POVERTY
YOUR EDUCATION
DEATHS
PRISON
In time, EVERYTHING WILL BE ALRIGHT.

Trust in the Lord,
Lean not to your own understanding.
Everything is going to be alright.
He'll never leave you without a plan
for your journey,

He will MAKE A WAY OUT OF NO WAY.
He will MAKE FRIENDS OF YOUR ENEMIES.
He will DUST YOUR MIND and CLEAR your heart.
He will GIVE you a job and PEACE OF MIND.
TALK to him, PRAY to him and TRUST him.

EVERYTHING IS GOING TO BE ALRIGHT!!

November 24, 2018

grl

I WANT TO THANK YOU

I WANT TO THANK YOU!!
I WANT TO THANK YOU!!
I WANT TO THANK YOU, THANK YOU, THANK YOU
FOR MY EYES,
FOR MY NOSE,
FOR MY EARS,
FOR MY MOUTH…
Thank you!

I WANT TO THANK YOU!!
I WANT TO THANK YOU!!
I WANT TO THANK YOU, THANK YOU, THANK YOU
FOR MY HANDS,
FOR MY HEART,
FOR MY LEGS,
FOR MY FEET…
Thank you!

I WANT TO THANK YOU
I WANT TO THANK YOU,
I WANT TO THANK YOU, THANK YOU, THANK YOU-
FOR EVERYTHING

November 25, 2018

grl

I WANT TO BE CLOSER!!

(Sing to the Tune of “Are You Sleeping”)

I

I WANT TO BE CLOSER .. I WANT TO BE CLOSER,
TO-OO GOD ……………TO-OO GOD
HOW DO I DO IT? .... HOW DO I DO IT?
PRAY, PRAY, PRAY……………. PRAY, PRAY, PRAY

II

I WANT TO BE CLOSER……I WANT TO BE CLOSER
TO-OO GOD…………………….TO-OO GOD,
HOW DO I DO IT? .... HOW DO I DO IT?
READ, READ, READ ……….. READ, READ, READ.

III

I WANT TO BE CLOSER … I WANT TO BE CLOSER
TO-OO GOD ……………………. TO-OO GOD
HOW DO I DO IT? .... HOW DO I DO IT?
LOVE, LOVE, LOVE ……….. LOVE, LOVE, LOVE!

April, 2019

grl

DON'T JUST DO YOUR PART IN LIFE!!

Just do your part,
Just do your part,
Just do your part,
It's not enough.

Be kind and take that extra step.
Extra, extra, extra, step
Be kind and take that extra step
And make it better for you and me.

No one can do it all alone.
Why don't you help and make things better?
No, I'll sit, wait to be asked.
Yes, I'll sit, and wait to be asked.

Your love, your opinion, your assistance will help.
It's not one person's job.
Just do your job and one extra step.
Will make a difference.
You'll see!!

October 6, 2018

grl

THE MASK

Mask, mask…Everywhere….
I go home and take it off.
Who am I?
Am I confused? What part will I play today?
"Hee, Hee"
That's survival!!
It's the portrayal of who you want me to be,
As you see me.
I pass you at work, I see you at play, I see you everyday.
I don't usually look like this-
I may be calling out for help.
So much is going on,
Who should I be today?
TAKE OFF THE LAYERS AND LAYERS AND LAYERS OF LIFE.

When I go home,
Do you see me?
Layers and layers and layers and layers…
My state of mind,
My survival to win…
Do you actually know who I am,
Do I know who I am?

.

Layers and layers and layers and layers…
Stop the medication,
Stop the stress,
Stop the depression,

Layers and layers and layers and layers…
Stop the medication,
Stop the stress,
Stop the depression,
Stop the prejudice!!
Layers and layers and layers and layers…
DO YOU KNOW WHO I AM?

November 24, 2018

grl

Section Two
Don't Forget to Pack a Little Kindness

"TREAT EVERYONE WITH
KINDNESS AND
RESPECT,
EVEN THOSE WHO ARE
RUDE TO YOU
NOT BECAUSE THEY ARE
NICE,
BUT BECAUSE YOU ARE."

-Unknown

BEING KIND

What Does It Mean to be KIND?

It means reaching out from inside.
To smile at someone,
To share what you have,
To cheer for someone who has tried.

Kindness can mean spending time with someone
who's feeling alone.
Inviting a person to play on your team
Or
Doing kind deeds on your own.
Kindness can change someone's mood or add
happiness to one's day.
No matter how simple the kind things you do,

THE JOY THEY GET GOES A LONG WAY.

grl

TRY A LITTLE KINDNESS, MY FRIEND

Do you see them over there?
Will you help them up the stairs?
TRY A LITTLE KINDNESS MY FRIEND,
TRY A LITTLE KINDNESS MY FRIEND!!

Open the doors.
Say, “yes mam”.
TRY A LITTLE KINDNESS MY FRIEND,
TRY A LITTLE KINDNESS MY FRIEND!!

DON’T SHOUT!! DON’T POUT!!
DON’T HIT OR THROW A CHAIR!!
Try a little kindness my friend.
Try a little kindness my friend.

grl

Section Three

Adventures Along the Way

MY TRAVELS TO AFRICA
DAKAR, SENEGAL
THE GAMBIA

de L'Intérieur
SPÉCIAL DE KARANG
POLICE

My Adventures in Africa May 9, 2024 - May 18, 2024

African Naming Ceremony, Abdoulaye Diablo Chief Village of Bonaba.

TRAVELS

I.

Miles and miles I go,
Years and years I go back,
To see my life,
My Love,
My Broken heart.

They left behind a civilization of warriors,
Of carpenters,
Of griots,
Of leaders,
Of politicians,
Of builders of humanity and souls of our people.
Miles and miles away.

But now, look at the school kids.
Look at those who are not going to school
Will they succeed? —how sad.

grl

II.

"Come into our market place.
Don't Stand Out There.
You buy it. Won't cost you much,
Come in, don't stand out there –
We make in your motherland."

Bowls, cloth, bracelets, shoes, pens, statues,
masks, clothes, scarves of their culture

III.

Get up in the morning and eat, eat, eat.
Wait for Jay and Mikel to tell us what to do,
Tell us where to go,
Tell us who we are
"Bonjour", "Comment allez-vous".
"We, we", "Yes, yes."

Up and down the bumpy road we travel.
No signs, no lights
Oops, did you see that,
Wow, that was close!

grl

IV

Walking with the lions, enjoying their play.
“Swish”, sounded the monkeys
grabbing their nuts and flying away.
Crust-back crocodile and goats, goats, goats!

What an experience!
What an adventure!
In Our Motherland.

May 16, 2024

grl

SOUNDS FROM THE MOTHERLAND

Dakar, Senegal and The Gambia

"TOOT, Toot", said the taxi.

"Meow, Meow" said the cat.

"Hee, Haw", said the donkey.

" Cock-a-doodle-do", said the rooster.

"Ruff,Ruff" said the dog.

"Chee, Chee," I'm your friend.

"Come Right In!"

May, 2024

grl

The “Door of No Return” in the house of slaves on Goree Island, Senegal

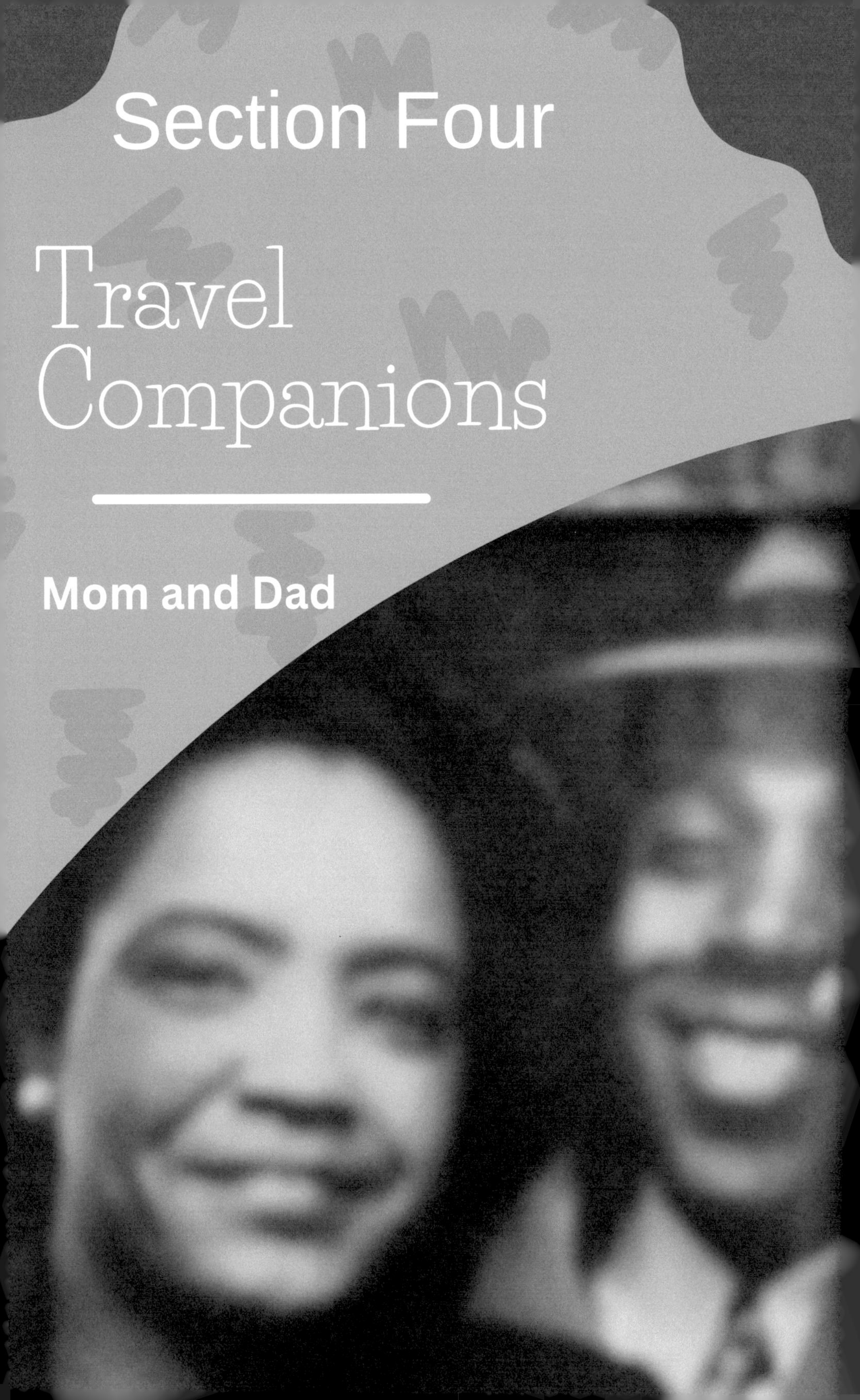

Section Four

Travel Companions

Mom and Dad

Bruce and Pennet, my brother and sister-in-law

BRUCE

I was such a bratty sister.
"Mama, mama, he's bothering me",
"He hit me."
"He's hitting my dolls."
Such a bratty sister I was.

Was it worth it?

Years go by
Life changes us as we grew up
Media and T.V. announcer, I did.
He now says proudly,
"Guess what every body,
That's my sister."

I wanted to be like you, BROTHER.

I WANTED YOU TO LIKE ME TOO!

grl

PENNET

So nice,

So helpful,

Many friends, friends, friends,

She always gave her time.

She always gave her last.

When you succeed

She would always say

THAT'S GREAT! YOU DID IT!

grl

CALLET

You're the daughter I never had.

Always there-

Morning, noon and night.

Auntie, Gwen, I will be a teacher, too.

Listen, I have something to say,

Two times a day.

CAN I TALK TO YOU!

grl

ODE TO A PHENOMENAL YOUNG LADY

"Walking in the sands of time"

He carried you all the way.
Nobody made it easy
Never pitted, never discouraged.
Our lives will never be the same
As we remind ourselves from whence you came,
Inspiring, educating others to move on without delay.
What lessons do you leave?
Don't stop,
Move on,
Hold your head up,
"THIS TO SHALL PASS"

AYISHA (life) ADIA (gift from God) EMMANI (faith) ASHFORD

St. Regis Hotel,
Detroit, Michigan 2014
grl

LETTER FROM YOUR DAUGHTER

From Gwendolyn Warren Lewis to
Carrie Lee Gibbs Warren

I'm carrying your burden in my belly.
You never told me the burden that you carried
made you feel disrespected, embarrassed and less
than human.

Yes, I saw you look down when you walked pass
the white woman. I also saw you step on the grass to
allow another to pass.

"Why did you do that?", I fussed.
You never gave me an answer.
I was upset with you.

You never explained your motives for your submissive
and embarrassing behavior.

Little did I know.
For the survival of you and your family
You had to look down.

But Mama, I won't look down.
I will always look up
FOR YOU, PAST GENERATIONS AND FOR ME.

grl

JOHN HENRY WARREN

My Daddy
1901-1990

You was there with me through thick and thin
With your STARE that taught me Right from Wrong.
You placed me in many arenas to perform
Speaking at teas, weddings and concerts.

You always gave good advice.
“Don't Fret,
You are smart like everybody else.
President Kennedy was a “C” average student
It's okay that you make one.”

He said he was born in the wrong time, the year 1901.
That he had many talents but THEY wouldn't allow him to show.
He would say that no man was better than him.
He who had travelled from Eufala-Clayton, Alabama.

He walked amongst Detroit's finest,
The NAACP, Westside Human Relations Council
and the Nacirema Club.

In every child's eye in the neighborhood
He was a tall man.
Every year he SWOOSHED them up
And land them in Belle Isle Park for a day full of
food and fun.

That's MY Daddy!
I won't forget his words of wisdom, his laugh
And his STARE that taught me RIGHT from
WRONG.

August, 2024

grl

WHAT DO I SEE?

(Dedicated to Joseph Alan Lewis)

What do I see?
I see a boy...Not I saw a boy
Wishing, anticipating ...not wishing hoping
Trying to survive.
Where do I turn?
Which way do I go?
"Trust in the Lord with all your heart,
Lean not to your own understanding"
There is so much untruth that you must sift thru…
READ, STUDY, PRAY…
You'll find the way.
Open your eyes to those around you, but know inside
what you are all about.
We cannot make others over.
Just do your part.

March 12, 2021

grl

KEEP SMILING

(MY ROAD RUNNER, JOSEPH BYRON LEWIS)

Keep SMILING!
You inspired ME.
You inspired EVERYBODY.
You helped us in EVERY WAY.
PATIENCE, PATIENCE, PATIENCE
LISTENED, LISTENED, LISTENED.

To ALL we had to SAY.
Not an enemy ever declared,
Survived by those who loved and CARED.
“STOP, LOOK AND LISTEN”, HE SAID!

July 3, 2024

grl

Section Five

Meet the Poet

Author's Biography

A personal message from the author
GWENDOLYN REGINA WARREN DUDLEY LEWIS

I live in Redford Township, located west of Detroit, Michigan. My formal education includes a Masters of Science in Library Science (M.S.L.S.) from Eastern Michigan University; Edu. Sp. in Administration from Wayne State University. These educational tracks led me to a 38 year career of media specialist librarian and staff coordinator in The Detroit Public Schools.

My need for creative growth led me to many media projects which placed me in the position that I am in today. Some projects included: writer of public service announcements at Channel 56; hosting the television programs, "Sounding" and "For My People".
I also hosted my own radio program, "Plant A Seed Read" at station WGPR which was a take off to my parent literacy guide, Plant a Seed Read...101 Activities To Motivate Children To Read. I was a motivational speaker and founder of "Hold On To Your Dreams" motivational speaking, with Les Brown as my mentor.

You ask what am I doing today? I am an Interactive Storytelling and Ambassador of Family Literacy as I entertain at festivals, schools and civic organizations. I am a national competitive race-walker; a student of American Sign Language; and a theatre and garden enthusiast. I also dabble in the kitchen.

I am thankful for my spiritual guidance from Tabernacle Missionary Baptist Church- Detroit, where I've been a member for over sixty-two years. Also I thank the Detroit Association of Black Storytellers, Detroit Story League and Toastmasters International for giving me my confidence, communication skills and stage presence throughout my journey.

I am a mother of one son, Joseph Alan Lewis. I am blessed with a host of friends and relatives.

"If you act like a winner, people will treat you like one and give you every opportunity to achieve."

-Adele Schelle.

grl

Booking Information

Contact Information for speaking engagements and performances

Gwendolyn Lewis,
Poet, Speaker & Interactive Storyteller

Visit my website: Gwenstoryteller.com
Email: Glewis2@mi.rr.com

Additional copies of the book are available on:
Amazon.com

Made in the USA
Columbia, SC
11 October 2024

43495505R00038